ECLECTIC LIVING

ECLECTIC LIVING

Ideas for Creating Your Own Unique Home Style

BARI LYNN

with Abbe Aronson

HarperCollins*Publishers*

HarperCollins books may be purchased for educational,
business, or sales promotional use. For information please
write: Special Markets Department, HarperCollins
Publishers, Inc., 10 East 53rd Street, New York, NY
10022.

FIRST EDITION

Interior photographs by Bari Lynn.
Step-by-step photographs by Ronald Capobianco.
All frames courtesy of Bed, Bath, and Beyond.
Cover photograph by Quentin Bacon;
hair by Frankie Foye; makeup by Susan Houser.

Designed by Joel Avirom and Jason Snyder
Design assistant: Meghan Day Healey

ISBN 0-06-019117-1
98 99 00 01 02 ❖/RRD 10 9 8 7 6 5 4 3 2 1

*This book is dedicated to my mother, Ellen,
whose elegant and graceful way of living
has taught me so much.*

CONTENTS

Acknowledgments *ix*

My Words *x*

Minor Cosmetic Surgery for the Home

Window Treatments
8

Colorwashing
12

Painted Rugs
18

Decorative Tiles
24

Crackle Finish
30

Simple Bed Canopy
34

Gold-Leaf Finish
40

Architectural Objects:
Incorporating Them
into Your Home
46

That's Entertainment!

Heat Transfer Linens
56

Gossamer Napkin Liners
62

Stitchless Table Runners
66

Etched Glass
72

Odd Containers for
Floral Arrangements
80

Floral Wreath or Centerpiece
86

Beaded Napkin Rings
94

Sugared Fruit Tiers
and Fruit Centerpieces
100

Great Gifts to Give and Receive

Picture Frames
112

Mosaic Serving Trays
118

Decoupage
124

Herbal Bath Oils
130

Embellished Candles
136

Gift Baskets
140

Gift Wrap
146

Herb Swags
152

Flavored Vinegars
158

Glossary of Terms and Tools *163*

Resource Guide *173*

ACKNOWLEDGMENTS

It's almost impossible for me to express my gratitude to all the friends, family, and colleagues who have contributed their time, love, and support, which enabled me to turn my dream into a reality.

To my family: my mother, Ellen, my father, Warren, and stepmother, Terry, thank you for giving me the wisdom, courage, and desire to embrace life with a unique eclectic vision. Special thanks to my brother Philip for his many hours of wise and needed counsel. To my love, Larry, whose humor, patience, understanding, and generosity allowed me to just be myself through a period of great change and wonderful new beginnings in my life. To Melissa Farris, my incredible assistant, whose enthusiasm, joy, dedication, and tireless work has meant more to me than she'll ever know, thank you.

My heartfelt gratitude also goes to Ronald Copobianco, technical photo adviser extraordinaire and my dear friend. To Abbe Aronson, whose vision, support, belief, and wonderful way with words brought this book to life. To Melissa Dunst, Kathleen Friery, and Jackie Leo, who knew that there was more to it than just the "Holiday Entertaining Series" at *Good Morning America*. To Sarah Maizes, my agent, who regularly watched my segment on *Good Morning America* and saw the potential so clearly and made this book possible. To Anthea Disney and Joseph Montebello, whose dedication and belief in this project allowed it to become my total labor of love. To Michael Trapp for welcoming and allowing me to photograph his magnificent home and shop, which has always been an incredible source of inspiration. To Joel Avirom and Jason Snyder, whose beautiful design made my photographs and words speak for themselves. To Liana Fredley, whose patience and hard work enabled us to meet deadlines. To Samantha, Max, and Taylor Levy, three special children who have given my life a new sense of joy.

I'd also like to thank Jennifer Kadonoff, Susan Houser, Frankie Foy, Quentin Bacon, Darienne Sutton, Tim Braun, Pam Pfeifer, Ted Kruckel and everyone at Ted Inc., Daphne Shirley, Anthony West, Peter Halbauer, Michael Carlisle, Ken Ross, Vicki Haupt, Dan Donachie, Kevin Cosgrove, David Whitacre, Laren Stover, Robin Gruber, Randy Gruber, Cynthia Jakeway, Dr. Mark Rogers, Meghan Day Healey, Bob and Naomi Schwartz, the entire Levy family, Jane Holzer, and Selma Bernstein for being a very special part of my life and this book.

MY WORDS

Let's take an informal poll. Do you consider decorating your home an overwhelming endeavor? Do you think you need a lot of money and time to *really* decorate your home the right way? I'm about to shatter your illusions.

The truth of the matter is this: You can turn your home into a beautiful, personalized haven, keeping budget and time constraints in mind. *Eclectic Living* gives you step-by-step directions for projects that will beautify your surroundings. And each project is illustrated with photographs that will spark your creativity. You'll be motivated to begin and successfully complete projects that you, your family, and your friends will enjoy for years to come.

I'd venture to say that your day is built around carpools, piano lessons, ball practice, and errands—or you're a corporate demon. Maybe your life is based on both extremes. Doesn't matter—you're pretty busy. You're always saying to yourself, "If only there were one more day in the week, I could really fix up my home." To make things simpler, I have chosen projects that are quick (half an hour to three hours, max), easy to do, and inexpensive. Whether you make them family activities or solo projects, you'll have a great time in the process and take pride in the results. Get ready for plenty of "Wow! Look what I did!" moments.

I want to emphasize that you don't need any special artistic ability or skills with tools to complete any of the projects in this book. In fact, using the most basic tools found in any hardware, art supply, or craft store, you'll sail through these projects with flying colors. It's all here: a shopping list for each project, a store guide, a glossary of terms, and a handy resource list for any of those harder-to-find items. Simple? You bet!

Don't be timid—go for it! *Eclectic Living* is broken down into Minor Cosmetic Surgery for the Home, That's Entertainment, and Great Gifts to Give and Receive. Browse through this book and let yourself be inspired to:

◆ Turn an old wooden stool that's been sitting in your garage into a new, crackle-finished masterpiece worthy of your living room.

◆ Transform your table linens, from standard to spectacular with nothing more than a hot iron and a little imagination.

◆ Create herbal bath oils and flavored vinegars that look store-bought but are in fact handmade with love.

Your home will look *better* than anything you've seen in some glossy magazine spread because it will have your own personal touch. *Eclectic Living* is about basking in the pleasure of being your own architect, your own designer, your own party planner, and even your own gift source.

It doesn't matter if you rent an apartment or own a house, or if your taste is gilded opulence, simple country rustic, or something in between—*Eclectic Living* has something for you. You will get a fresh perspective on the use of space, the still-life effect of different objects placed together, the impact of color, texture, and shape. With these concepts in mind, take another look at your home. Pick a section, pick a project, and get busy—you're ready to begin.

Bari

WHERE TO GET WHAT YOU NEED

You may have some questions about where you can purchase supplies needed for a project. Each item needed to complete any of these projects has a letter next to it indicating where you can buy it.

For example, needlenose pliers will have an **H** and a **C** alongside it, telling you that this item can be found at a home improvement store or craft store. Here is a list of dingbats.

Art supply store .... **A**

Craft store .... **C**

Fabric store .... **B**

Floral supply store or flower shop .... **F**

Hardware store or home improvement center .... **H**

Home decorating or linen superstore .... **M**

ECLECTIC ESSENTIALS

Some items—like scissors, tape, and iron and ironing board—I'll assume
you have around the house. But take a look at my list of *Eclectic
Essentials*. These are the items you should keep handy for any project.

- *Scissors*

- *Tape measure*

- *Ruler*

- *Pencil, pens, felt-tip markers, erasers*

- *Scotch tape*

- *Standard white glue*

- *Hot-glue gun*

- *Spray adhesive*

- *Inexpensive large and small paintbrushes*

- *Needlenose pliers*

- *Screwdrivers—Phillips and regular*

- *Hammer*

- *Rubber gloves*

- *Sponges*

- *Protective goggles*

- *Iron and ironing board*

- *X-acto knife*

- *Old newspaper, old sheets, or sheets of plastic
  (to use as drop cloths)*

ECLECTIC
LIVING

MINOR
COSMETIC
SURGERY
FOR THE HOME

This is the part of the book where you take your *fantasy* and turn it into *reality*. These are quick decorating tips that can change the entire tone of a room.

We tend to forget that the simple things like *color*, *texture*, and *details* can really bring a room to life and give it its own identity. For example, images taken from old books, photographs, and postcards can make a kitchen or bathroom into a

work of personal expression. The gentle use of
color in our colorwashing process can introduce
warmth and subtleties to your walls, making them
seem old and weathered in the best possible way.
And a simple bed canopy can make it seem as if
you are sleeping in your own royal palace.

Room "staples," like window treatments and
rugs, have never been so easy to create. Standard
bedsheets become billowing draperies. Plain

woven sisal rugs become personal pieces of art (this project is so simple, even the kids can customize their own floor coverings).

And going back in time, we'll use architectural objects such as old windows, doors, and facades, and ancient processes like gold-leafing that work just as well today.

We're going to cover a range of techniques and styles in this section, bringing a sophisticated

yet pure eclectic style to your way of living.

Whether you live in a new condo, loft apartment,

or traditional Colonial home, you will certainly

find something in "Minor Cosmetic Surgery for the

Home" that will make your life more beautiful.

WINDOW TREATMENTS

Got sheets? Great. We're going to create inexpensive window treatment using basic bedding. You can start with new goods or use the old standbys already in your linen closet; just be sure they're in presentable condition and that they are evenly colored with no discernible stains or markings. Depending on the width of your window, if you want a lot of gathers, you'll need four flat twin-sized sheets; if you want fewer gathers, use two queen-sized sheets.

WHAT YOU NEED

*For 1 window (2 panels): 4 flat twin-sized sheets
(2 per panel) or 2 flat queen-sized sheets* Ⓜ

Tape measure Ⓗ

Scissors

Iron and ironing board, or a suitable surface

Stitchless glue Ⓐ Ⓒ

*Curtain rod, curtain brackets, screws, and screwdriver
or power drill (depending on the type of wall)* Ⓗ Ⓜ

1. Measure the length of the window and decide how long you want your draperies. Do you want them to "puddle" on the floor, or do you want them to end at the top of the windowsill? The wide hem at the top of the sheet will form a casing for the curtain rod.

2. Cut the sheet at the bottom to the desired length, leaving ¼ to ½ inch for the bottom hem. Make a hem: Fold the edge under and press with the iron to form a proper crease. Apply a thin layer of stitchless glue on the inside of the hem. Press the hem with the iron.

3. Trim ¼ inch off each side of the finished top portion of each sheet. Slide the curtain rod through the casings from end to end.

3a

4. Position the brackets, screw them to the wall, and hang your new curtains!

3b

4

COLOR-WASHING

If you stop to think about the time people spend within the four walls of their living room or den, surely they must notice the paint peeling or cracking on these walls through the simple passing of time. Not to worry. I've got a simple solution that doesn't involve many coats of primer and paint: colorwashing. A colorwash is made from latex (water-based) paint; use eggshell-finish paint in a color that complements or contrasts with your furnishings. It's easy to create an antique-looking, uneven texture to the wall, and the paint dries relatively quickly.

WHAT YOU NEED

Plastic drop cloth ⓗ

Fine (no. 400) sandpaper ⓗ

Spackle and putty knife ⓗ

Mixing sticks ⓗ

1 quart latex paint ⓗ

Gallon-size pail or container ⓗ

Glycerine (pharmacy or drugstore)

1 quart water

4- to 5-inch paintbrush ⓗ

Clean rags (for making pattern)

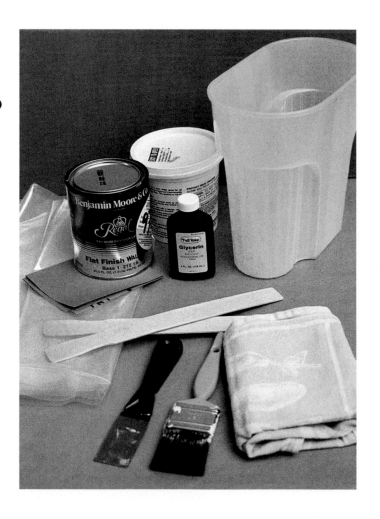

1. Cover the entire area very well with the drop cloth to protect your floors and fixtures.

2. With fine sandpaper, gently sand doors and door jambs to create a slightly rough surface so that the colorwash adheres to it.

3. Prepare the walls for colorwashing: Scrape and sand away any peeling paint and fill in cracks with spackle, using the putty knife. Let it dry and sand again with fine sandpaper to smooth out lumps and bumps in the spackle. Fill deep cracks a second time if necessary and repeat sanding process.

4. Prepare the paint mixture: Stir the paint in the can to completely mix it; pour 1 quart of paint into the gallon pail. Add 1 tablespoon of glycerine, which will make the mixture easier to work with, and

4a   4b

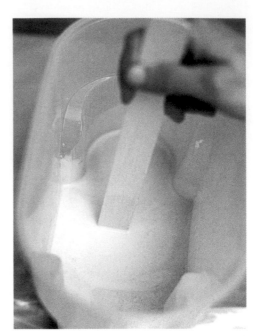

4c

4d

1 quart of water. I like to start with less water and dilute paint further if necessary. Mix thoroughly.

5. Now you have your colorwash ready for application to walls. With
the paintbrush, apply the wash from ceiling to floor. This is the fun
part. Dip your brush into the wash, then "slap" the color loosely and
irregularly in all directions, trying to avoid heavy brushmarks. After
you do this, you can gently "rag" the wall to assist in the antiquing
process. Dab a clean rag all over the surface in an irregular pattern.

5a

5b

6

6. When the first application is dry (in about 2 hours), repeat the process. Be sure you have thoroughly covered the area with a drop cloth. Don't be alarmed if a very watery wash runs off in the beginning. Don't expect the desired effect after only one coat. The second coat makes a miraculous difference.

AND ANOTHER THING . . .

I happen to prefer light colors and pastels for colorwashing. If you are using a wall that is not white or light-colored, remember to choose shades that will complement the base color already there. This is a colorwash, not a heavy application of paint.

PAINTED RUGS

How often do you replace your carpeting? Not too often, I'd bet. But wouldn't it be great to have seasonal area rugs that you could change on a whim for next to no money, especially in high-traffic areas like children's rooms or the hallway, or on the porch or in the mudroom. Here is a way to do it, using a sisal rug in a natural color and your choice of designs and colored enamel spray paints. Jute and coir (coconut-husk fiber) rugs are also usable, but can be inferior in quality.

WHAT YOU NEED

Paper and pencil

2 plastic drop cloths **H**

Tape measure **H**

Sisal rug in desired size **M**

Wide felt-tipped markers **A** **C**

2-inch-wide masking tape **A** **C** **H**

Scissors

Assorted colors of enamel spray paint (Spray paint should be used only in a well-ventilated area such as an open garage, backyard, or rooftop.) **A** **C** **H**

Graphics you'd like to use: stencils, star template, etc. **A** **C**

Liquid Leaf paint **A** **C**

Small artist's paintbrush **A** **C**

1. First, sketch your design on a piece of paper. Better to make a mistake here and correct it than on the actual rug. In the photos, I'm creating a rug with two thick stripes on either end and a star pattern in the middle section.

2. Cover the work area with a drop cloth.

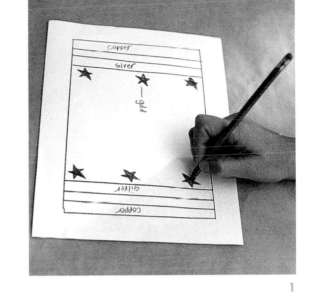

1

3. Using your tape measure, come in a few inches from the edge of the rug. Make a mark with your marker on the rug to indicate the thickness of the stripe. Then apply a strip of masking tape across the width of the rug where the stripe ends. Be sure to press the masking tape firmly down to keep the paint from seeping underneath the tape.

3a

3b

4.   Measure, mark off, and apply tape to create the boundaries of your
      second stripe. The sisal that is covered up by the masking tape sep-
      arates the stripes.

5.   Repeat Steps 3 and 4 at the opposite end of the rug.

6.   Cover the closest exposed area of the rug with a piece of cut-up
      dropcloth and tape it down for good measure. Spray away! I'm
      using copper spray paint. Let it dry for 10 to 15 minutes, then apply
      a second coat of paint.

6a

6b

7.   When the first stripe is dry, cut a
      piece of drop cloth and cover the
      stripe with it. Then put another
      piece of drop cloth over the middle
      section of the rug, next to the sec-
      ond stripe where the masking tape

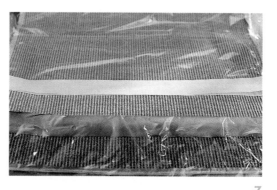

7

      stops. Now you can spray-paint the second stripe. I'm using silver
      paint for my second stripe. Again, let it dry for 10 to 15 minutes
      and apply a second coat.

8.   Repeat Steps 6 and 7 at the opposite end of the rug.

9. Remove the pieces of drop cloth and peel away the masking tape, and the stripes are revealed.

9

10. If you'd like to add some other element to the pattern, take a stencil (I'm using a star), trace the outline with your marker and then fill in the form with the Liquid Leaf.

10a

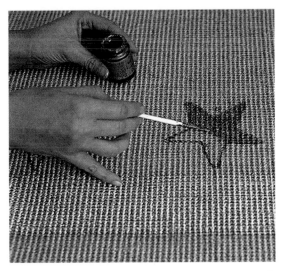

10b

AND ANOTHER THING . . .

Look for rugs that have been treated with Scotchguard so that they are stain-resistant. If the rug you purchase isn't pretreated with Scotchguard, buy a can yourself, apply it, let it dry, and then proceed with painting.

DECORATIVE TILES

Like to spruce up the kitchen or bathroom for a few dollars? It's easy with glass tiles and your favorite images. You can use flowers, portions of old letters or any kind of correspondence, newspaper or magazine articles, old photos or stamps, whatever you'd like. You can alternate the image with tiles made with solid-colored paper in a coordinating color—rice paper is always effective. This project is especially attractive if the exposed wall space over your sink or counter is in less-than-perfect condition or simply boring and crying out for a change. And, as you'll see, you're not married to these images forever.

Mod Podge is a water-based acrylic glue and sealer that is predominantly used in découpage. It's easy to use, fast-drying, and odorless.

WHAT YOU NEED

To tile a 48-by-32-inch backsplash:

Any desired images, and photocopies of the images

Solid-colored paper Ⓐ Ⓒ

77 (4-by-4-inch) glass tiles with quick-seam edge finish, ⅛ inch thick Ⓗ

X-acto knife Ⓐ Ⓒ

Mod Podge (an acrylic sealer/glue) Ⓐ Ⓒ

1-inch paintbrush Ⓐ Ⓒ

Glass cleaner and paper towels

Tube of silicon tub and tile sealer Ⓗ

WHAT YOU DO WITH THIS STUFF

1. Measure the area you will be tiling. Say you have a 32-by-48-inch backsplash area behind your sink or underneath your kitchen cabinets. You will be leaving a 2-inch border on all sides of the backsplash area, so you will need to cover a 28-by-44-inch area with tiles, a rectangle 7 tiles tall by 11 tiles long, or a total of 77 tiles.

2. Select your image and your solid-colored paper.

3. Make photocopies of the image, being sure to size the copies so the image fits on a 4-by-4-inch glass tile.

4. Place one of the photocopied images under a tile and use the X-acto knife to cut out the image so it fits perfectly under the tile. Make sure you use a new, sharp blade to achieve a clean cut.

2

4

5a   5b   5c

5.   Apply Mod Podge to one side of the tile, place the image on the glass, image-side down, and smooth out the wrinkles. When it's dry, apply a layer of Mod Podge to the back of the paper and let it dry.

6.   Repeat Steps 3 and 4 with the solid-colored paper and glass tiles. You'll use these solid-colored tiles to alternate images and create a checkerboard design on the wall.

7.   After all the glass tiles are prepared, clean them with glass cleaner to remove smudges.

8.   To mount the tiles, apply silicon sealer to the back of the paper on each tile and press onto the wall, leaving a 2-inch border on all sides of the backsplash area. The silicon renders the tiles mildew- and water-resistant. Leave about ¼ to ⅛ inch between the tiles.

7

8a

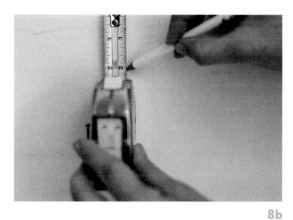

8b

8c

AND ANOTHER THING . . .

After a few years, you may want to change images. Just remove the tiles with a putty knife, peel the images off, and clean up the tiles, and you can start all over again.

CRACKLE FINISH

Do you admire the look of the crackled glaze on old porcelain and pottery? Here's a way to achieve that "yesteryear" look on furniture. It's inexpensive and, best of all, nontoxic, so it leaves behind no nasty fumes. Not only is it great for furniture, you can use this crackling process on mirrors, picture frames, candlesticks, tabletops, old boxes, humidors, even flower pots. In this project we will apply a crackle finish to a piece of furniture (in the illustrations I'm using an unpainted wooden bar stool). If your furniture has been finished, lightly sand it before applying the acrylic paint. Most craft stores sell crackle kits and small bottles of acrylic paints (so there is no waste) in a wide variety of colors—everything from pastels to metallic finishes.

WHAT YOU NEED

Drop cloth **H**

Piece of furniture

Two colors of acrylic paint, one for the base and a contrasting color for the crackle design **C**

Three 1- to 2-inch paintbrushes **A** **C**

Crackle Medium (manufactured by Plaid, makers of Mod Podge) **C**

Hair dryer (optional)

WHAT YOU DO WITH THIS STUFF

1. Completely cover the work area with the drop cloth.

2. Paint the furniture with the base color. Let dry for 30 minutes.

3. Apply the Crackle Medium with your second paintbrush. Let dry for 30 minutes or follow the instructions on the label.

4. Using the third paintbrush, apply the contrasting color acrylic paint. Watch as the crackle finish appears before your eyes!

3

2

4

AND ANOTHER THING . . .

Want bigger cracks (as opposed to smaller, veinlike cracks)? Take your hair dryer, using the cool setting, and hold it 6 inches away from the drying paint, moving the dryer up and down the length of the furniture.

SIMPLE BED CANOPY

Romantic? Definitely. Dramatic? Positively. Expensive? No way! Every little girl dreams of sleeping under a canopy bed, and many grown-ups *still* long for a canopy bed but simply don't have the room for it. This canopy bed is the answer to all your prayers. It's easy to put up, easy to take down and clean, and even easier to change seasonally with different fabrics. Anything from muslin to an elaborate damask will work. The only requirement is that your bed must be against the wall to make this canopy work. Sweet dreams.

WHAT YOU NEED

Pencil

*3 drapery swag holders that mount onto the wall
(you may have to buy 2 sets of 2)* Ⓜ

Screws for swag holders and screwdriver Ⓗ

Fabric (instructions below on how to measure your fabric) Ⓑ

Iron and ironing board

Stitchless glue Ⓐ Ⓒ

1. To establish position of the canopy, find the center of the bed or the bed's headboard. The canopy should be centered over the bed, but it doesn't need to be mathematically exact. At the centerpoint, go "up" the wall and make a small mark where you want the canopy to begin. The higher you go up on the wall, the more dramatic the canopy and the more fabric you need. Mount 2 of the drapery swagholders on the wall, 2 inches from each side of the top of your headboard or the edge of your pillows.

1a

1b

2. Now mount the center drapery swagholder on the wall where you made that small mark with your pencil.

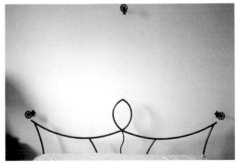

2

3. Create the canopy. Do you want the canopy to "puddle" on the ground or do you want it to simply graze the floor? Here's the formula for estimating how much fabric you need: Start at the point on the wall where the canopy will begin and measure straight down to the floor. Multiply that figure by two and then add two more yards for good measure. Voila!

4. Create a hem at either end of the fabric. Fold up a ¼- to ½-inch hem and press with the iron to form a proper crease. Apply a thin layer of stitchless glue inside the hem. Press the hem with the iron.

5. You're ready to hang your canopy. Gather the fabric *widthwise* and, holding the middle of the fabric, wrap it once around the center tieback, securing the fabric. The ends will cascade down to the floor. Loosely wrap each side around the respective swag holder. Don't wrap any of the fabric so tightly that it is stiff and forms sharp angles. You want the canopy to drape softly from the top drapery swag holder down to the side swag holders.

Stylist's tip: If the fabric cascading down from the center drapery swag holder to the side swag holders looks flat and lifeless, add bunches of paper tissue inside the folds to give the canopy some oomph.

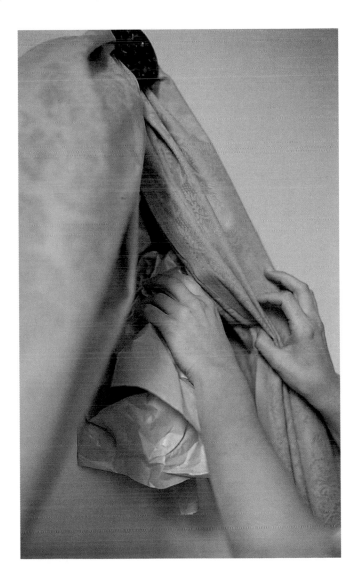

GOLD-LEAF FINISH

Gold-leafing is an ancient art form, traditionally used to decoratively finish picture frames and fine furniture in European palaces—think Baroque. Gold leaf is, in fact, *actual gold* pounded into very fine sheets. It's incredibly thin—in some gourmet circles, it's even applied to luxury foods and eaten. (If you want to try this at home, make sure you use pure 22-carat gold.) Other grades of gold on the market work just fine for leafing your home-decor items. Artificial (or composite) gold sheet leafing is also available—don't turn up your nose at it. It's actually easier to work with than real gold. You can apply gold-leaf to just about anything—picture frames, ceramic or terra-cotta flower pots, mirrors, boxes, and furniture.

A WORD OF CAUTION

This process takes a bit of time and is not for the person who needs to see results in five minutes. I also wouldn't attempt this project while preparing lunch for the kids. The gold-leaf sheets are so thin that if they are blown on too strongly, they can tear and disintegrate. If you are new to gold-leafing, start with a small item such as a picture frame or small mirror before tackling a larger or more important piece.

WHAT YOU NEED

Picture frame or small mirror

Wunda Size (a water-based adhesive) Ⓐ Ⓒ

1-inch paintbrush Ⓐ Ⓒ Ⓗ

Badger-bristle paintbrush Ⓐ Ⓒ

Booklets or sheets of gold leaf (enough to cover item) Ⓐ Ⓒ

WHAT YOU DO WITH THIS STUFF

1. Make sure the surface of your item is clean and free of dust.

2. Apply Wunda Size evenly with the regular paintbrush. It should dry to the
   appropriate "tack" in 15 to 30 minutes
   and it will hold its tack for up to 36
   hours. The tack should feel dry to the
   touch, but sticky, like dried spilled apple
   juice. If the tack is too wet, the gold leaf will shrivel; if it's too dry,
   the leaf will not adhere to the surface.

2

3. Gently touch the badger-bristle brush to a sheet of gold leaf, lift-
   ing it out of the booklet or off its base paper. This may take some
   practice.

4. Apply the sheets one by one, side by side,
   to the object, overlapping slightly until
   the entire surface has been covered.

4

5. When the entire object is covered, use
   your finger to gently smooth down the
   leaf, or gently brush the leaf with the
   badger-bristle brush, setting all the sheets in place.

6. If you are working with a large surface area, it may be necessary
   to work in small sections, so that the Wunda Size doesn't dry completely. This is a long process, but the results are incredible.

ARCHITECTURAL OBJECTS: INCORPORATING THEM INTO YOUR HOME

First things first: This is not a precise "how-to" project. This is more about creating a style or ambiance completely unique to you. The design and architectural elements that decorated

the buildings of yesteryear just aren't used in new buildings anymore. But all of the smaller, individual elements that defined those styles—the finials, the balusters, the columns, even old door knobs—can be put to use in new homes, which usually lack architectural details.

My good friend Michael Trapp, the owner of an incredible antique store that doubles as his home in West Cornwall, Connecticut, has captured the essence of the Old World style, while at the same time giving it a fresh, eclectic twist. I've always admired his style and was pleased to be able to shoot this part of my book in his amazing shop and home.

Michael uses peeling wooden finials that most people would think of as garbage to create simple still lifes, nestling them next to old velvet armchairs for an enchanting effect.

He takes garden elements such as large clay pots and old garden urns and uses them indoors to set a mood. He utilizes them as stand-alone objects of art and as planters in the traditional sense. In his view, these pots and urns can be just as striking when they are empty as when they are holding dried fruits or leaves.

Michael uses columns everywhere, made out of cement, marble, wood, and even tin. Some of these columns support large plants, but others are randomly placed, not only to fill empty spaces but to add architectural interest where none existed before.

I also love the way he incorporates small marble, bronze, or cement statues in his table settings, in place of floral centerpieces. Bear in mind that to achieve this look you don't have to work with antiques or expensive statues. In fact, I like the look of a grouping of old finials on a table, and I'm always on the prowl for them at yard sales and flea markets. To take this one step further, I've seen wonderful reproductions of these items at home superstores and departments stores in the decorative-accents section.

THAT'S
ENTERTAINMENT!

Have you ever been to a wedding,
gala dinner party, or some other
social event where all the details were just perfect?
The flowers, the lighting, the place settings . . .
Everything seemed so right, in fact, that the whole
atmosphere became even *more* elegant, *more*
serene, *more* lush. Perhaps you've seen photos of
some fabulous celebrity soirée or perhaps you simply have a vision in your head of an ideal bridal

shower or a dinner for two. You probably thought, "I could never do this on my own in my house."

Yes, you can. And you will.

You don't have to be a party planner to create a beautiful ambiance. You just need to remember that the key to any lovely room or setting lies in the details, and in this section you'll learn all my secrets for taking eclectic elements and combining them for elegant entertaining.

Here, you're going to learn how to embellish your dining table, your sideboard, and your coffee table with nature's bounty—outdoor elements that will look elegant, not artificial. You'll learn how to liven up linens and glassware with decorative touches that can evoke any number of moods. You'll learn how to work with fruits, flowers, and leaves to create beautiful centerpieces that cost pennies. And if you're tired of your own dishes or serving pieces, you'll be able to incor-

porate fabulous finds from flea markets and tag sales into drop-dead table accessories that will look as if they came from the most expensive store in town.

Everything you'll learn here is so simple, yet it will enhance your presentation tenfold, whether you choose to undertake one project at a time or several all at once. This time, it will be your guests that come away thinking, "I'd love to be able to do that in my home!"

HEAT-TRANSFER LINENS

Wouldn't it be great to dress up a plain table with images that mean something to you? Any of us can buy new table linens with the traditional frills and flowers and bows, but think how much more you would enjoy your table if the design elements in it were personal to you. Are you an Anglophile? How about proper teacups and saucers as a theme? Are you a bona fide nature boy or girl? How about insects, fresh from the meadow? A sports fanatic? A world traveler? The point is, anything is possible when it comes to table dressing, thanks to the wonderful world of copy centers. The other secret is heat-transfer paper, the stuff that is used to transfer images onto

T-shirts. Most local copy shops carry this paper. Yes, if you can make a special color copy of it at one of those convenient copy centers, you can show it off on your table!

WHAT YOU NEED

Images from books, magazines, postcards (here's where you get creative)

Scissors

Photo heat-transfer paper (copy shop)

New or used cotton, linen, or poly-cotton table linens in a light color **M**

Iron and ironing board

WHAT YOU DO WITH THIS STUFF

1. Select the image or images that you'd like to use—I'm using teacups, but feel free to use any images that appeal to you. Decide how many you will need for your linens, napkins, etc. You also can enlarge or reduce your image at the copy center.

2. Cut the images out, cutting as close to the images as possible. Don't worry about being completely exact.

3. Have the images copied onto photo heat-transfer paper at your copy shop, which should cost a few dollars. If you space the images efficiently, you can put lots of images on one piece of photo heat-transfer paper. If your copy shop doesn't stock the photo heat-transfer paper, purchase it at a craft shop or photo supply shop and bring it and the images to the copy center.

4. Cut the images out of the photo heat-transfer paper.

5. Now prepare the table linens. Make sure they are clean and free of dust, and iron them to remove any moisture or wrinkles. (Iron each napkin right before you are ready to work with it.)

6. Take the cut-out images and place them image side *down* on the table linens (the paper on the back will be peeled off after you iron). You can position the image anywhere on the linens. For napkins, I like to put

6

the image on the diagonal on one or all four corners, so I would prepare 4 or 16 images for 4 napkins. With placemats or table-cloths, where you put the images should depend on what part of the linens show when you set the table.

7. Turn the iron to maximum heat but *no steam*. Iron over the paper back of the image, using pressure. Run the iron back and forth over the cutout for about 60 seconds.

8. Remove the iron and let the image remain on the fabric for about 15 seconds before peeling off the paper and throwing it away. If the image starts to stick and won't peel, run the iron over the paper side *only* and try again.

7

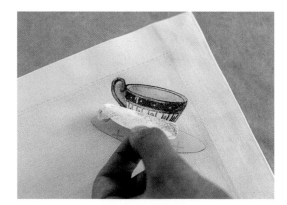

8

AND ANOTHER THING . . .

If you are using an image that incorporates words or letters, ask the copy center to "mirror" the image, so that when you iron it onto the linens, the words and letters read correctly, not backward.

If you are using multiple images per napkin, make sure that you leave enough space in between each one—if the iron accidentally touches an image as you are applying another one, the image will smear and leave residue on the iron. It doesn't matter if you've just applied the image or if the image is five years old. Once you've applied the image, keep the iron away, and iron only on the reverse side of the linens.

Here's the best part about this project. Just like T-shirts, these linens can be subjected to normal use and repeat washings. The image will remain intact for at least a few years. This project would also work well on pillowcases, draperies, and even cocktail napkins.

GOSSAMER NAPKIN LINERS

Layers and layers of lovely linens create a dramatic dressed table, but who has the money to keep buying and buying? The solution: napkin liners that allow you to dress up your practical linens anytime. Napkin liners are not particularly functional, but they really add an extra dimension and sparkle to the table. If you choose a sheer fabric for your liners, you can breathe life into several sets of table linens whenever the spirit moves you. Personally, I like metallic liners, which coordinate with black, white, pastels, holiday colors, etc. You can also mix and match the liners, which will give you a lovely array of golds, silvers, coppers, and pearls on one table.

WHAT YOU NEED

Sheer organza fabric,
1 (19-by-19-inch) square per liner,
one for each napkin **B** **C**

Iron and ironing board

Stitchless glue **A** **C**

Cloth napkins and rings

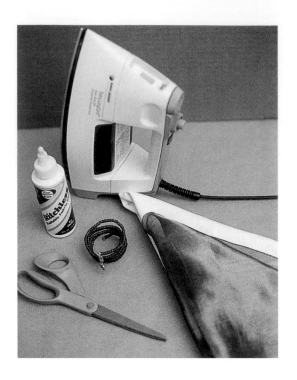

WHAT YOU DO WITH THIS STUFF

1. Take a square of fabric and fold up a ¼- to ½-inch hem and press with the iron to form a proper crease. Repeat on all four edges of the fabric.

2. Apply a thin layer of stitchless glue inside the hem. Press down on the hem with the iron. Repeat on all four sides of the fabric.

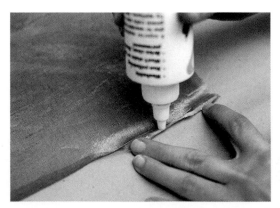

1

2

3. To create a finished edge, apply another thin layer of glue to the inside edge of the hem and fold the hem over on itself. Press down on the new finished seam with the iron. Repeat on all four sides of the fabric.

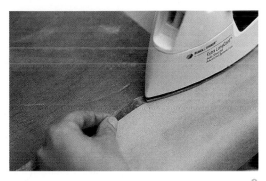

3

4. Now you're ready to use the liners. Place it over your napkin. Grab the napkin in the middle and slide through your napkin ring holder.

AND ANOTHER THING . . .

Gossamer is delicate and should be dry-cleaned, or at least hand-washed. But remember, since the liners rarely come into contact with food, they won't need to be cleaned very often.

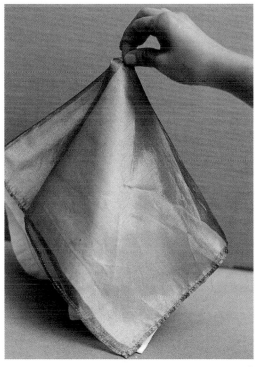

4

STITCHLESS TABLE RUNNERS

Remember how your mother and grandmother had their "good table linens"? You'd see them fanning the tablecloths out or placing the table runners at the beginning of every holiday as they prepared to set the table and you just knew something wonderful was going to happen. Well, let's face it, how many special, formal occasions do you host in your home? The fact of the matter is that most of us entertain very casually; putting the take-out Chinese food onto your everyday dishes instead of eating out of the cartons constitutes a "special occasion" for many of us, and often the table "linens" of choice are paper.

But this need not be the case. How about some super-quick, stitchless table runners that will transform your dining experience into something really terrific in minutes? These runners are easy to make and can work well in any room of the house; with the proper fabric, you can create a great runner for any end table, nightstand, or pedestal.

WHAT YOU NEED

Tape measure

Scissors

Any fabric (a heavy brocade is nice for the holidays) Ⓑ

Stitchless glue Ⓐ Ⓒ

Iron and ironing board

WHAT YOU DO WITH THIS STUFF

1. Measure the length of your table, and add 12 inches on each end for overhang. The runner should be at least 12 inches wide; it can be wider if you'd prefer.

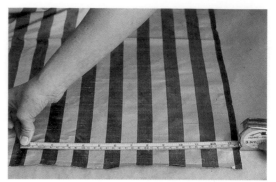

1

2. Measure and cut the fabric. Fold up a ¼- to ½-inch hem and press to form a proper crease. Repeat on all four edges of the fabric.

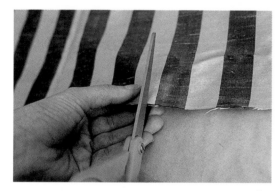

2a

2b

3. Apply a thin layer of stitchless glue inside the hem. Press the hem with the iron. Repeat on all four edges of the fabric.

3

4. To create a finished edge, apply another thin layer of glue to the inside edge of the hem and fold the hem over on itself.

   Press down on the new finished hem with the iron. Repeat on all four edges of the fabric.

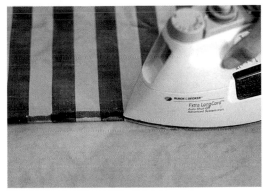

4

5. Admire the finished product! Drape your new runner over your table and pat yourself on the back.

AND ANOTHER THING . . .

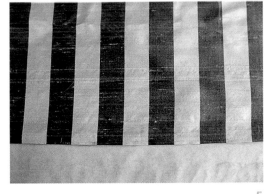

5

If you want to get even more creative, you can embellish the corners of your runner with charms. Just stitch them on with ordinary thread and then wash with care (perhaps use a mesh lingerie bag).

ETCHED GLASS

Etched glass is really an art form. Consider the French jeweler and glassmaker René Lalique, who made etched (or "frosted") glass famous. Now don't get nervous just because I'm invoking the name of a famous French glass designer. What's important to remember is that you can create beautiful etched pieces right at home, using a technique called "acid cream etching," which employs diluted hydrofluoric acid in a cream form to eat away the shiny surface layer of the glass.

It's incredibly easy and you can use almost any kind of glass, with the exception of tempered glass (specially treated for windshields or shatter-proof windows or mirrors) because it's not strong enough

to take the acid. You can use mirrors, window panes—you name it!—but what's really popular right now are martini glasses and cocktail shakers.

WHAT YOU NEED

Protective goggles

Rubber gloves

Plain glass item (I use a cocktail shaker and martini glass) **M**

Denatured alcohol **H**

Sponge **H**

Spray mister **H**

Clean cloth or paper towel

Masking tape **A** **C**

Stick-on vinyl letters to form SHAKE **A** **C**

24-ounce bottle of Armour etch cream (you can etch your way around the world with this size) **A** **C**

Soft-bristle paintbrush **H**

WHAT YOU DO WITH THIS STUFF

1. Begin by suiting up with your goggles and rubber gloves. Thoroughly clean the shaker with a solution of ¼ cup denatured alcohol and ½ cup water. Double or reduce the recipe as needed. Use a sponge or put the mixture in a spray mister bottle and mist away. Wipe with a clean cloth or paper towel and allow the glass to dry.

2. The trick is to cover the parts of the glass that will *not* be etched. My cocktail shaker will have an etched band surrounding the word "SHAKE," and I'm using masking tape to create a border for the band. I'll write the word with simple stick-on letters.

    Run a strip of masking tape completely around the shaker.

    Run another strip of masking tape around the shaker about 2 inches below the first. Note to Perfectionists: Sometimes it takes a few tries to get the tape around the shaker evenly, but you'll get the hang of it.

2a

2b

3. Apply the letters to form "SHAKE" between the strips of tape. Once the tape and letters are in place, make sure that you apply enough pressure to make them adhere completely to the glass, so that the acid cream doesn't seep underneath the tape; once the cream is applied you can't make corrections.

3

4. Apply the acid-etch cream with the paint-brush. The cream has the consistency of peanut butter and you should to spread it on in a thick layer.

5. Leave the cream on for 1 minute or follow the instructions on the jar. You'll know your shaker is ready when the cream starts to bubble slightly. Rinse it under cool water, using your sponge and wearing those gloves—we're working with acid here and you need to protect your hands.

4

6. Peel off the tape and letters. Don't panic if you can't really see the frosted effect when the glass is wet. When it's dry, it looks terrific!

6

7. For the martini glass, clean as described above. Apply masking tape in straight strips that begin at the top of the stem and run up to the rim. Apply the acid cream and proceed as described above.

7a   7b   7c

AND ANOTHER THING . . .

For "bubble" martini glasses, use loose-leaf paper reinforcements applied in rows or columns; I like curvy, swirling rows to mimic real bubbles. Just apply the acid-etch cream to the hole in each reinforcement and you'll create a charming procession of rising bubbles! Looks great on champagne flutes too.

ODD CONTAINERS FOR FLORAL ARRANGEMENTS

Did someone say "odd"? Well, yes, odd is good. I mean, *really*, the traditional vase or basket, while being very pretty, is a little predictable. What about using a terrific old urn from the garden, a fountain basin, an antique glass or metal bowl? The idea is to create a personalized floral arrangement that doesn't look as if it came from a store. Now is a great time to make use of some of those flea-market finds. You liked it, you bought it, now here's what you can do with it.

WHAT YOU NEED

*Urn, bowl, or other container large enough
to hold the floral tape grid described below*

¼-inch floral tape or masking tape **C** **F**

*Dried or fresh flowers and leaves, a combination
of taller blooms and shorter, full flowers (in the photos,
I'm using hydrangea and eucalyptus)* **F**

Scissors

WHAT YOU DO WITH THIS STUFF

1. If you're using fresh flowers, fill the container with water first. Dry the edges. Attach strips of the floral tape to the container, forming a grid across the top. The strips should be 1 inch apart and should extend over the sides of the container by about ½ inch. The bottom layers of flowers will hide the tape.

1a

1b

2. Cut the flowers to the appropriate height for your container. Fill the holes in the grid with flowers, using taller blooms in the center. The trick is to support each flower with another. The flowers you place in the middle of the grid may tend to droop or drift off to the side, but as you add flowers, the "team effort" will keep them all upright.

2

3. Surround those taller blooms with small full flowers, which will cover the gaps left in the grid.

4. Fill the outer edges of the grid with bunches of leaves that will cascade down the sides of the urn and cover the floral tape.

4

FLORAL WREATH OR CENTERPIECE

Before anyone chimes in with "Sleighbells ring, are you listening . . ." I'm telling you up-front that wreaths are not just for the holiday season. In fact, these beautiful wreaths are made with gorgeous spring flowers that have absolutely nothing to do with dashing through the snow in a one-horse open sleigh. The basis is the Oasis wreath, a wreath made of a dense, absorbent sponge material (Oasis brand) used by florists. You can make these wreaths with any type of seasonal flowers, but springtime tulips, daffodils, freesia, orchids, and roses turn these wreaths into masterpieces. And these wreaths are not just for your everyday table, but can be used for weddings and buffet

tables. They work wonderfully because the flowers are not overwhelmingly large (you can see across the table to your dining companions, even if you add small, wide pillar candles as centerpieces), and the smell is heavenly.

WHAT YOU NEED

Green floral wire **C** **F**

Oasis wreath **C** **F**

Branches, leaves, and vines (for filler) **C** **F**

Floral water tubes, 3 to 4 inches long, with pointed ends **C** **F**

Small to medium flowers of your choice **F**

Scissors

Tall pillar candle (optional) **C**

WHAT YOU DO WITH THIS STUFF

1. This wreath can be hung on the wall or laid flat on the table for use as a centerpiece. If you want to hang the wreath on the wall, wrap the wire around the Oasis, and then twist the ends together into a loop. Or you can use the wreath as a centerpiece flat on the table.

1

2. Begin by laying the filler—leaves, branches, and vines—on top of the wreath in a sweeping motion, all going one direction. Eyeball the arrangement before you push the stems into the Oasis. Once you think the filler looks nice, push the stems into the Oasis.

2a

2b

3. Fill the floral tubes with water. Cut the flowers to the desired length and put them into the tubes. If the stems are thicker than the rubber opening on the cap of the tube, cut an X into the opening with your scissors. Smaller flowers can be gathered into bunches and held in one tube.

3a

3b

4

4. Arrange the flowers in the wreath, pushing the ends of the tubes into the Oasis. The leaves, branches, and vines should hide the floral tubes. Add more filler if necessary.

5. You can leave your wreath to dry naturally, especially if you are using roses, small sunflowers, mums, or hydrangea, or you can replace the flowers and water as necessary.

6. If you will be using the wreath as a centerpiece, put the pillar candles in the center.

AND ANOTHER THING . . .
CUT-FLOWER PRESERVATION TIPS

◆ When cutting fresh flowers, cut the stem on the diagonal, which allows water to travel up the stem more easily.

◆ To help preserve your flowers, combine a tablespoon of bleach with a gallon of water and use this water to fill your tubes.

◆ Keep your cut and arranged flowers out of direct sunlight, preferably in a cool spot.

◆ Add fresh water daily or as needed.

BEADED NAPKIN RINGS

Think of a beautiful, romantic restaurant . . . The waiter pulls out your chair and whips a large and luxurious napkin out of its elaborate ring holder before draping it on your lap. Pretty swell. Guess what: Beaded napkin rings are supereasy to make, add grace to the meal, and, depending on your room lighting, become little twinkling points around the table, especially when they are decorated with fanciful charms. But they needn't be fussy just because they are exquisitely delicate. First choose the charms you want to use, then choose complementary beads; you can use any beads, as long as they will slide on 20-gauge wire.

WHAT YOU NEED

To make 4 napkin rings:

About 3½ yards 20-gauge wire in gold or silver, whatever color better suits your beads **C**

Scissors

Needlenose pliers **H** **C**

A medium-sized bag of beads (1 hank) **C**

Small, thick jump rings (for attaching charms) **C**

Small charms with loops **C**

Cardboard toilet tissue tube

WHAT YOU DO WITH THIS STUFF

1. Measure and cut the wire 24 to 32 inches long. The longer the wire, the more loops the napkin ring can have.

2. With your needlenose pliers, grasp the wire and wrap it around the tip of the pliers two or three times. This forms a loop that will hold the jump ring, which in turn holds the charm.

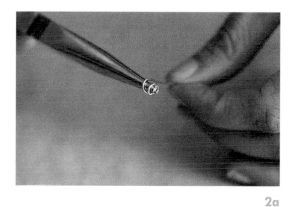

2a

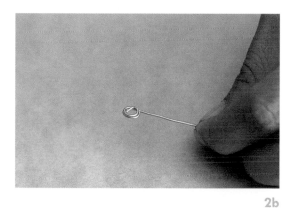

2b

3. String beads onto the wire, leaving ½ inch at the end of the wire.

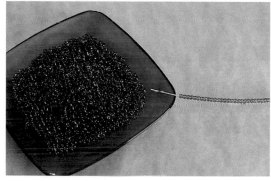

3

4. With your needlenose pliers form another loop, as small as possible, smaller than the first loop—its purpose is to hold the beads in place as a "stopper."

5. Attach the jump ring to the larger loop and then attach the charm to the jump ring.

4

5

6. Holding the charm against the toilet tissue tube, wrap the beaded wire around it to form a spiral. The wire is rigid enough to hold its shape when the roll is pulled out.

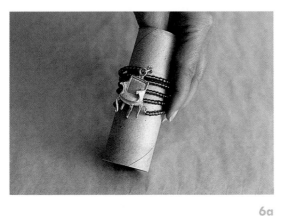

6a

6b

AND ANOTHER THING . . .

When you set your table and use the napkin rings, the charm should dangle down over the center of the ring, as illustrated in the photo.

SUGARED FRUIT TIERS AND FRUIT CENTERPIECES

Most of us keep fruit around all the time; we force the kids to have an apple after school or slice a banana onto our cereal in the morning. But fruit can also be used as decoration. Dressed up with a glittering layer of sugar, fruit makes an incredibly beautiful centerpiece in almost no time. Use as much fruit as you need to make an abundant presentation; apple, pears, lemons, limes, mandarin oranges, cranberries, and grapes are best. And the gorgeous display will last up to a week!

WHAT YOU NEED

Pastry brush or 1-inch paintbrush

Fruit with skin

3 to 6 egg whites, lightly beaten—keep extras on hand just in case

2 cups of sugar

1 or 2 cookie sheets

A tiered serving tray, pedestal cake plate, or any favorite serving piece—glass, wire, or metal looks best

Sprigs of herbs

WHAT YOU DO WITH THIS STUFF

1. With the pastry brush, glaze each piece of fruit with egg whites. The fruit should be glossy but not dripping.

2. Either roll the fruit in sugar, or sprinkle the sugar directly onto the glazed fruit. Don't worry if you miss some areas; it's pretty when the sugar isn't evenly applied.

1

2

3. Place the sugared fruit on the cookie sheet to dry, making sure that the pieces don't touch.

3

4   5

4. When the sugar coating is dry, arrange the fruit on the serving
    piece. Pyramids and layered arrangements look best, and if you've
    made too much fruit, you can do a smaller platter for your coffee
    table or bar area.

5. Insert the herb sprigs into the arrangement to fill in any blank
    spaces between the fruit.

    Remember: Once sugar-coated, this fruit is not edible, as the raw
    egg whites could harbor salmonella.

AND ANOTHER THING . . .

A pedestal punch bowl with fresh fruit would also be terrific here. Use lots of moss—you can reuse it again and again. Then, just pile on your washed fruit. Don't make the presentation too high; little hands or clumsy guests will knock over your handiwork.

GREAT
GIFTS
TO GIVE
AND RECEIVE

To me, these projects are about shortcircuiting buying expensive gifts. All over the country, you can walk into any store, even clothing stores, and find novelty home items for sale: vases, lotions and potions, gourmet food baskets. The trend of giving gifts for the home is more popular than ever, but if you can give a gift that you've made with your own two hands, it simply makes the present that much more special.

In "Great Gifts to Give and Receive," you'll
find wonderfully creative presents to whip up
for birthdays, holidays, dinner parties, or any
occasion when a really personal gift is essential.
I think presentation is very important—no
cellophane, plastic wrap, or the usual curling
ribbon here! You'll be using beautiful fabrics,
raffia, dried leaves, and gorgeous decorative
bottles. It will be clear to the recipient from the

moment you hand over the gift that you had her
(or him) in mind as you made it.

These gifts are wonderful luxuries that the
recipient might not think of indulging her- or him-
self in: bath oils, candles, fragrant herb swags,
along with picture frames and serving trays that
your friends will enjoy for years to come.

Of course, there is a downside to being a mar-
velous gift giver . . . Once word gets around that
you're handing out these wonderful gifts, you'll be
very, very busy. Every hostess in town will start
inviting you over!

PICTURE FRAMES

Photos capture those precious, personal moments, but unfortunately, when it's time to frame your pictures, the options are often impersonal—and expensive. It's easy to personalize plain picture frames and we're going to look at three basic customized frames: the flowers forever frame for the romantic at heart, the fallen leaves frame for the sophisticated crowd, and the rubber ducky frame for the kiddies. Remember, though, you're limited only by your imagination, in terms of the types of embellishments you choose. Ribbons, charms, even dog bones—if you can hot-glue it or spray-stick it, it will work.

FLOWERS FOREVER FRAME

WHAT YOU NEED

Dried or fake flowers—as many or few as you desire **F** **C**

Scissors

Antique or plain inexpensive unfinished picture frame **C** **M**

Hot-glue gun **A** **C**

WHAT YOU DO WITH THIS STUFF

1. Trim the stems of the fake flowers as close to the blossoms as possible.

2. Place the frame flat on your worktable and arrange all of the flowers on the frame. This is a preview of what the frame will look like and will guarantee that you're not covering up the photo space with big petals or leaves. Sometimes less is more.

3. Use the hot-glue gun to attach the flowers one by one to the frame.

1

2

3

FALLEN LEAVES FRAME

Use a stainless-steel frame and use spray adhesive to attach real dried leaves to the surface. I like to place the leaves on the corners.

RUBBER-DUCKY FRAME

Apply pastel-colored paint to an unfinished wooden frame. Let it dry, then use the hot-glue gun to attach small rubber ducks or any whimsical toys or items you wish.

MOSAIC SERVING TRAYS

You're sitting around your home, tearing your hair out as you try to dream up something special that will add a little sense of the exotic to your dinner party, which is right around the corner. Or you are expected at a dinner party this weekend and you've already given this hostess the usual flowers and wine on several previous occasions. The remedy: a mosaic tray! It's a great way to use charming old ceramic pieces—the more colorful the better. Buy old stuff at flea markets or use the odd plates and serving pieces around the house (the ones that you don't have the heart to throw out). A mosaic tray is easy to make, beautiful, and so practical.

WHAT YOU NEED

Protective goggles H

Gloves

3 or 4 medium-sized pieces of old china or ceramics (plates, platters, pitchers, or flower pots)

An old towel

Hammer H

Tile cutter (optional) H

Cookie sheet with a ¼- to ½-inch rim

Hot-glue gun A C

Premixed tile grout H

2- to 3-inch putty knife (optional) H

A few damp rags

Steel wool H

WHAT YOU DO WITH THIS STUFF

1. Put on the goggles and gloves and smash the china: Place the china or ceramic piece on your old towel, fold it up, and use the hammer to safely break the china into fragments. Weed out the curved pieces and save the flatter ones. Hint: You can use a tile cutter to break the china into small pieces.

2. Arrange the pieces in any desired pattern on the cookie tray, colored side up (and sharp side down if there is an edge). Swirls and circles and any kind of geometric pattern are nice—get creative.

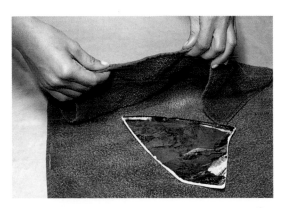

1a

1b

1c

2

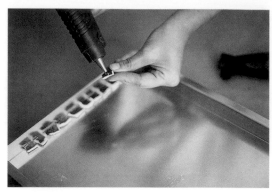

3a

3b

4a

4b

3.   Stick the pieces to the cookie tray with the hot-glue gun and let
     them dry.

4.   Smear the premixed tile grout over the cookie tray and work it
     down into the gaps between the china pieces. You can use the putty
     knife or your fingers. Don't pile on too much grout—you can
     always add more. Your goal is to fill the gaps right up to the tops of
     the china pieces, smoothing the grout to form a relatively flat and
     even surface. Use the damp rag to wipe excess grout off the top of
     the pieces so the color and pattern are exposed.

5. Allow the tray to dry for 24 hours. When the grout has dried, use steel wool to gently remove the excess grout from the sides of the tray, if necessary.

AND ANOTHER THING . . .

This is the kind of project that the whole family can really enjoy, especially the smashing. Obviously, use caution with small children and don't break up the china by dropping it from your second-story window. Keep your eye out for interesting cheap china and ceramics at flea markets or yard sales and you'll always have the pieces on hand the next time you want to make a tray. This technique can be used on everything from flower pots to tabletops to drinking-glass coasters.

DECOUPAGE

Decoupage, the art of decorating surfaces by applying cut-out designs that are then lacquered, is currently experiencing a big comeback. Decoupage is considered a fine-art form, and now it's easy to create using nontoxic water-based products that are simple to apply and dry to a clear, hard, durable finish. You can decorate large or small pieces of furniture, trunks, clocks, or even kitchen cabinets and stools. Children's furniture looks especially terrific when decorated with decoupage. You can use the technique to decorate common, unpainted wooden keepsake boxes or even cigar boxes. Before applying the cut-out designs you can cover the object you are decorating with solid-colored decorative paper.

Half of the fun is choosing the images you will use as decoration, but you might not want to be limited to just one shot at each image. Here's a great way to duplicate your image without spending a lot of money: Use a color laser copy machine found at most copy centers. This allows you to preserve your original image. You also can enlarge or reduce the image at the copy center. I've selected vintage postcards that my great-grandfather sent to my great-grandmother when they were courting to use for decoupage projects, as well as wrapping paper and greeting cards.

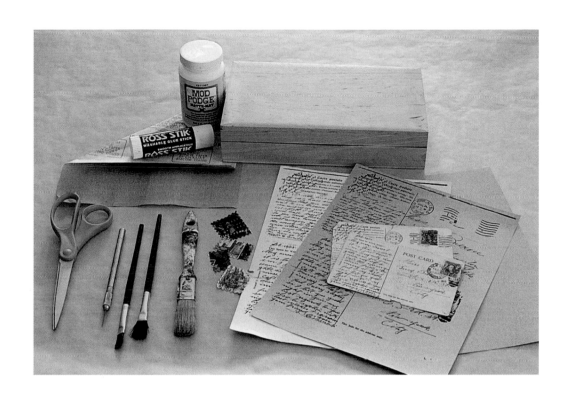

WHAT YOU NEED

Images you want to use

Small, sharp scissors or X-acto knife **A** **C**

Pencil

Box or other surface you want to decorate

Solid-colored paper **A** **C**

Mod Podge (an acrylic sealer/glue) **A** **C**

3 soft 1 to 2-inch paintbrushes **A** **C**

Fine sandpaper (no. 400) for wood **H**

Damp rag or cloth

WHAT YOU DO WITH THIS STUFF

1. Carefully cut out the images with the scissors or X-acto knife. Pay attention to detail.

1

2. Using a pencil, trace the outlines of the sides of the box onto the solid-colored paper and cut them out with scissors. Use Mod Podge to attach the paper to the sides of the box. Let it dry.

2a

2b

3. Using a soft paintbrush, apply Mod Podge to the paper covering the box. Place your images in the desired pattern on the box. In the illustration, I'm using one large postcard in the center of the box

3

and smaller ones around the outer edges. You also can layer smaller and larger images. Allow the glue to dry for 10 minutes, making sure the images are smooth and wrinkle-free.

4. Using a larger soft-bristle paint-brush, apply a thin coat of Mod Podge over the entire surface, brushing in one direction only. The Mod Podge acts as a sealer and protects against dirt and spills. Allow 10 to 15 minutes to dry.

4

5. Sand the dried Mod Podge with the no. 400 sandpaper to smooth out any brush strokes, and wipe the surface with the damp cloth. Coat with up to five layers of sealer. Utility items like tabletops and trays should get five coats for extra durability.

HERBAL BATH OILS

To paraphrase Robert Tisserand, "If it pleases the nose, it also pleases the spirit." So what could be better than naturally scented bath oils to give as gifts to those you love on Christmas, Mother's Day, or anytime? Bath oils are not a new idea; they have been around for centuries and today you can wander into any shopping center or mall and find whole stores devoted to lotions and potions.

But why buy them when you can create personalized fragrances for pennies and then bottle them in beautiful flasks and decanters to match the occasion?

While there are loads of oils on the market that energize the spirit, let's face it, most of us who get the chance to soak in the bathtub are seeking some

serious down time—we want to relax, not rev up! With that in mind, we're going to create a relaxing bath oil that you'll love so much you might want to keep some for yourself! The special oils in the recipe are all available at health food stores. Once you feel confident with this basic blend of oils, experiment. There are numerous books about aromatherapy that provide recipes for oil mixtures to soothe the soul, invigorate and heal the body, stimulate the mind . . . or put you in the mood. Try new oils, new scents. This is like a chemistry playset for grown-ups.

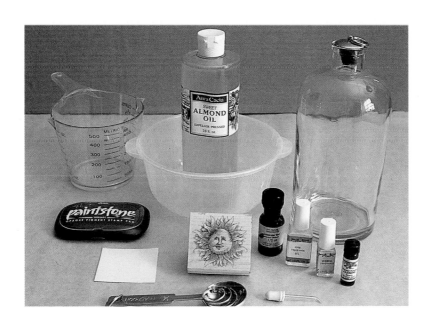

WHAT YOU NEED

To make 4 ounces of bath oil:

½ cup sweet almond or castor oil

Mixing bowl

Eyedropper **C**

*Essential oils of rose, lavender, jasmine,
and verbena (health food stores)*

Mixing spoon

Funnel **H**

Bottle or leakproof container with stopper top **M**

Rubber stamp, ink pad, and paper (optional) **C**

*Ribbons, dried flowers or dried fruit, hole puncher, glue,
and blank gift cards (optional)* **C** **F**

WHAT YOU DO WITH THIS STUFF

1. Pour the sweet almond oil or castor oil into the mixing bowl. These oils, so-called "carrier" oils, have no scent and are the base for our end product.

2. Using your eyedropper, add 10 drops rose oil, 10 drops lavender oil, 2 or 3 drops jasmine oil, and 2 or 3 drops verbena oil.

1

2

3. Mix well with a spoon.

4. Using the funnel, pour the mixed oils into the bottle and stopper it.

4

5. Now comes the fun part. You can embellish the bottle by creating a gift card that "announces" what's inside. Or you can use a rubber stamp with a decorative design to make a label and glue it onto the bottle. Or glue a few rose petals to the gift card, thread the card with ribbon using a hole puncher, and tie the ribbon around the neck of the bottle. This would work equally well with a spray of lavender or a dried lemon slice, since all three fragrances are incorporated into the oil itself.

5

EMBELLISHED CANDLES

Candles emit a soft, atmospheric light that enhances any room. Today, candles come in an assortment of sizes, shapes, and colors; especially popular now are those that are poured with flowers, fruit slices, and herbs already mixed into the wax—but they can be expensive. Here's a way to take a plain candle and dress it up for pennies; the tall, sturdy pillar candles work best. And these candles are *truly* unique! By the way, this process works wonderfully on scented candles, especially if you coordinate the scent with your embellishments (for example, a lavender-scented candle with fresh lavender wrapped around it).

WHAT YOU NEED

Cinnamon sticks, dried wheat, lavender, or other embellishments Ⓒ Ⓕ

Scissors

A tall, thick pillar candle or other basic candle Ⓒ Ⓜ

Raffia Ⓐ Ⓒ Ⓕ

WHAT YOU DO WITH THIS STUFF

1. Begin with the embellishments (I'm using lavender in the illustrations). Cut the stems so that they are all about one quarter the length of the candle. I'm using a 12-inch candle here, so the lavender is cut to a length of about 3 inches.

1

2

3

2. Tie 2 strands of raffia around the candle. Slip the lavender stalks underneath the raffia and go around the circumference of the candle with lavender, covering the candle entirely, so the lavender looks looks full and lush.

3. Trim off any excess raffia.

4. As the candle burns down, cut the stems so that they do not become a fire hazard.

GIFT BASKETS

It *is* the thought that counts, true, but why have your host or hostess thinking, "Gee, she went to a store and bought a gift basket. How original . . ." If a gift basket is what grabs you, it's much nicer to customize it for the recipient than to rely on what a store deems appropriate. I'm going to show you how to make two kinds of gift baskets, a "social tea" basket and a "hobby" basket. By keeping certain basic pointers in mind, you can create individualized gift baskets for anyone on your list. Trust me: The responses you'll get from the recipients of these highly personal gifts will thrill you. *Everyone* loves a gift that reflects his or her true passions.

ART-INSPIRED HOBBY BASKET

WHAT YOU NEED

Tissue paper or shredded paper **A** **B** **C**

Metal container or aluminum flower bucket **F**

2 to 3 small pads of paper **A** **C**

Small book on art masterpieces **A**

Loose paintbrushes, small box of paints,
small box of colored pencils **A** **C**

Raffia **A** **C** **F**

Fabric (optional) **B** **C**

WHAT YOU DO WITH THIS STUFF

1. Use the tissue or shredded paper to fill the bottom of the container and prop up the gifts.

2. Nestle the larger items toward the back of the container and place the smaller items in front. Use the raffia to tie loose items together.

3. If you want a more finished look, wrap the container in fabric.

1

AND ANOTHER THING . . .

Baskets are easy to use, but in some instances you should try to use a container that matches your gift basket theme. A gift for gardeners? Use a watering can or a

2

flower pot. For serious cooks, a colander or stockpot. For a pet lover, a fishbowl or food dish for Fido. For your favorite little guy, a dump truck.

SOCIAL TEA BASKET

WHAT YOU NEED

*Tissue paper, shredded paper,
and luxurious-looking fabric* Ⓐ Ⓑ Ⓒ

*A basket, any kind that appeals
to you (traditional, modern wire
basket, etc.)* Ⓒ Ⓜ

*Teapot and 2 cups and saucers
(mismatched flea-market finds are
original and charming)*

Tea towel Ⓜ

*Box of loose tea, butter biscuits,
small chocolates, and other
tea-time gifts*

*Large piece of sheer fabric,
cheesecloth, or shantung silk* Ⓐ Ⓑ Ⓒ

*Plenty of medium-width organza
or gossamer ribbon* Ⓑ Ⓒ

WHAT YOU DO WITH THIS STUFF

1. Use the tissue or shredded paper to fill the bottom of the basket and prop up the gifts themselves. Cover the tissue with a piece of luxurious fabric, like dupioni silk.

2. Nestle the teapot, cups, and saucers in the middle of the basket as the centerpiece, then surround with the tea towel and other gifts. If the goodies seem to be sinking, add more filler to the nest. The basket should appear overstuffed.

3. If the basket has a handle, wrap ribbon around the length of the handle. Tie bows at the two bases of the handle.

4. If you want to protect the contents of the basket while it's being transported, place the filled basket on the center of the large piece of fabric. Gather up the sides of the fabric and tie it up with ribbon.

GIFT WRAP

I don't know about you, but every time I stop by a paper or party store, I'm just dumbfounded by the prices for gift wrap! Sometimes the price is more than $10 for a roll of wrapping paper that will wrap only two or three boxes—and forget about fancy bows and gift boxes. Plus, most of it looks the same; not too many original ideas here. My suggestion? Approach wrapping in a simple way: use a solid craft paper or a simple wrapping paper and then embellish it with interesting, more personalized elements. Create a magical "still life" when you wrap your gift!

WHAT YOU NEED

Scissors and Scotch tape (for basic present wrapping)

Brown craft paper or simply designed wrapping paper **Ⓐ Ⓒ**

Ribbon **Ⓒ Ⓕ**

Raffia **Ⓐ Ⓒ Ⓕ**

Hot-glue gun **Ⓐ Ⓒ**

Paper or fabric leaves **Ⓒ Ⓕ**

Spanish moss **Ⓒ Ⓕ**

Artificial bird and nest **Ⓒ Ⓕ**

Small artificial bird's eggs **Ⓒ**

Gold or silver spray paint (optional) **Ⓐ Ⓒ**

WHAT YOU DO WITH THIS STUFF

1. Wrap the gift in the craft paper and tie it with ribbon, but don't make a bow.

2. Using 10 to 15 strands of raffia, tie a big loopy bow and leave lots of loose strands of raffia hanging down.

3. Hold the bow in the center of the package, allowing the excess raffia to cascade 2 inches over the sides of the package. Cut the raffia if it's too long.

4. With the hot-glue gun, attach one or two of the fabric or paper leaves to each end of the raffia strands.

5. With the hot-glue gun attach the bow to the center of the package and attach a small handful of Spanish moss to the center knot of the bow. This creates a base for the nest.

5a

5b

6

7a

7b

7c

6.   Attach the nest to the moss base, also using the hot-glue gun.

7.   The bird can perch on the side of the nest and will stay in place with a little hot glue. Fill the nest with a tiny bit of raffia or Spanish moss. The eggs go into the nest (I've spray painted mine gold and silver), also secured with hot glue.

AND ANOTHER THING . . .

If birds aren't your thing, you can use butterflies, ladybugs, or fireflies. You'll be able to choose from many items at the craft store. And if you want to abandon the nature theme, you can use regular ribbon instead of raffia and attach almost any small item.

Hint: Miniature children's toys work great with gifts for kids.

HERB SWAGS

This project will thrill those of you with a green thumb. Those of you who are *all* thumbs, you're in luck, too. Herb swags are terrific gifts, useful for cooking, wonderful as room fresheners, and *cheap* when you make them yourself. Back to you gardeners for a moment: Don't despair when the first frost comes and your herb garden withers away. Herb swags allow you to enjoy your hard work all year round. And for the rest of you, store-bought herbs work just as well.

WHAT YOU NEED

For a 3-foot-long swag:

6 to 10 bunches of fresh herbs, like bay leaf, rosemary, basil, tarragon, oregano, or lamb's ear (more bunches will make the swag fuller)

Plant clippers **C** **F**

Cookie sheet

Floral wire **C** **F**

3-foot raffia braid **F** **C**

WHAT YOU DO WITH THIS STUFF

1. Clip off 4- to 5-inch sprigs of the herbs and dry them out thoroughly. You can spread the cuttings out on the cookie sheet and air-dry the herbs for about a day and a half; you can dry the clippings in the oven at 200 degrees for 3 to 5 hours; or you can even microwave them on medium for 50 seconds to 2 minutes. When the herbs are dry, the stems will be hard. It's very important that the herbs dry out thoroughly to avoid mildewing after the swag is complete.

2. Gather the dried herbs into small bundles and use floral wire to tie them.

1

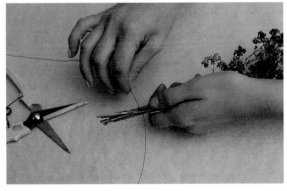

2

3. Attach the bundles to the raffia braid using the floral wire. You can create any number of "patterns" with the herb bundles, but it's easiest to create the swag with all of the stems pointing in

3

one direction. Or you can begin at one end of the braid with all the stems pointing toward the middle of the braid, and when you get to the middle, then switch the direction of the bundles. This will give you a "bowtie" effect, which looks great displayed or hung horizontally, perhaps on a mantle or over a door frame.

4. If you are hanging the braid, use the floral wire to make a loop on the back of the braid, threading the wire in and out of the raffia strands.

4

AND ANOTHER THING . . .

Dried herbs are more potent than fresh herbs, so the swag would be very useful in the kitchen. Just snip off what you need for your recipes and away you go. Try incorporating bundles of freshly dug garlic or a string of colorful hot peppers. You can even tie the swag into a wreath shape. A eucalyptus leaf swag would be heavenly in the bathroom, because the steam from the shower brings out the aroma.

FLAVORED VINEGARS

Flavored vinegars are growing in popularity and can be very costly in stores, so I'm passing on a great recipe that you can make at home. The decorative wax-sealed bottles make perfect gifts, and the color-infused vinegars look wonderful on the kitchen window sill. This recipe uses raspberries and lemon, but you can also use strawberries, blueberries, sliced mangoes and peaches, and orange rinds, in any combination you wish. Try using Japanese rice vinegar and adding a slightly crushed stalk of fresh lemongrass; or a couple of dried hot peppers with rice vinegar or white vinegar, omitting the sugar; or use a bunch of fresh herbs, substituting ¼ teaspoon of salt for the sugar.

WHAT YOU NEED

Rind of 1 lemon

1 cup fresh raspberries

Colander

Funnel

⅛ cup sugar

2 cups distilled white vinegar

Any kind of decorative bottle with stopper top Ⓜ

Beeswax Ⓐ Ⓒ

Double boiler

Ribbon, about ½ inch wide and 12 inches long Ⓒ Ⓕ

WHAT YOU DO WITH THIS STUFF

1. Cut the lemon rind into matchstick slivers.

2. Wash the raspberries and drain them in a colander.

1

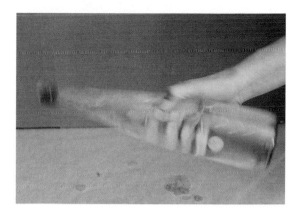

3a   3b   3c

3. Using the funnel, put the sugar and vinegar in the decorative bottle and shake the mixture until the sugar dissolves.

4. Fill the decorative bottle with lemon rinds and raspberries. Put the stopper on the bottle.

5. Melt the beeswax in the top of the double boiler.

4

5

6. Take the piece of ribbon and extend it from one side of the neck of the bottle, over the cork, to the other side. Holding the ribbon over the cork, dip the top of the bottle into the beeswax. Dip it in and out a few times until you have a thick layer of wax. When you or the lucky recipient of this beautiful gift want to open the bottle, you just lift the ribbon and break the seal.

7. The rest is up to Mother Nature. Put the bottle on a sunny shelf and let it sit and cure for about two weeks. Enjoy!

AND ANOTHER THING . . .

These vinegars are perfectly safe to make at home, since the acid kills the bacteria. Oils flavored with fresh ingredients, however, can be breeding grounds for botulism—stick to store-bought flavored oils.

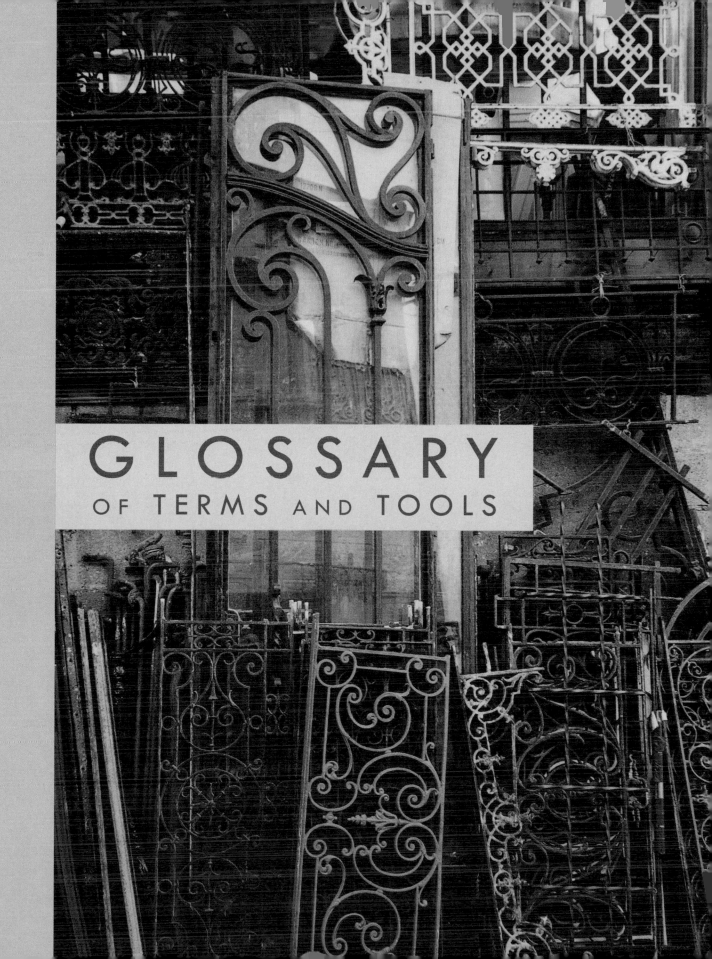

GLOSSARY
OF TERMS AND TOOLS

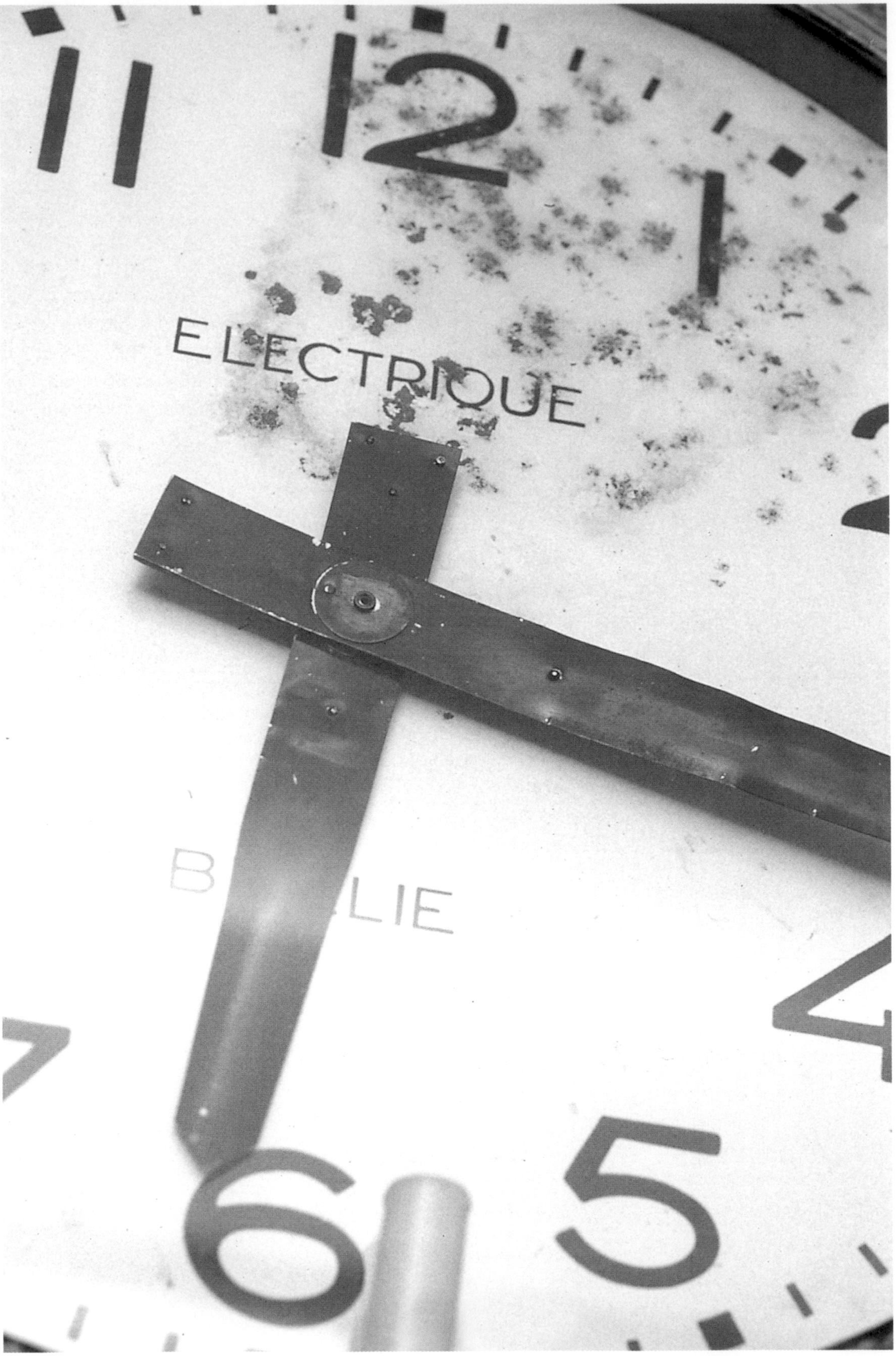

ELECTRIQUE

BUTCHER'S PAPER Like craft paper, except it has been bleached, and is used for wrapping meat. It makes a great plain paper base for stamped gift wrap.

CARRIER OIL A nonscented oil that acts as a base for essential oils when they are used to scent larger quantities of oil.

COLOR LASER COPY A technically advanced color copy process, done on a special laser printer machine, that results in realistic, sharp reproduction.

COLORWASH A mixture of latex paint thinned with water that is brushed on in layers. It can be manipulated by ragging, sponging, or rolling to create different surface textures.

CRACKLE GLAZE Decorative ceramic glaze developed in eighteenth-century France to reproduce the fine network of cracks found on Eastern lacquerwork and pottery.

CRAFT PAPER Inexpensive unbleached brown paper sold by the roll like wrapping paper. Great for gift wrap and as worktable drop cloth for projects.

DECOUPAGE A French word for the technique of decorating a surface with paper cutouts, which can be accomplished very simply with an acrylic sealer/glue called Mod Podge.

DENATURED ALCOHOL A product used as a thinner for shellac, as a cleaning agent for glass, and as a fuel for marine stoves. To make a solution to clean glass or porcelain, dilute one part denatured alcohol with two parts water.

ESSENTIAL OIL The pure essence derived from plants, herbs, and flowers in concentrated form.

FINIAL A decorative ornament that forms the terminal part of any projection, for example, the decorative ends of a curtain rod.

FLORAL TAPE A product commonly used by florists to make bouquets and grids. Found in craft and floral shops.

FLORAL WATER TUBES Plastic tubes filled with water, used to keep individual blooms fresh. The tube has a rubber cap with a small hole for a flower stem. For floral wreaths, purchase tubes with pointed tips.

FLORAL WIRE Thin green plastic-coated wire that wraps around the stems of flowers so you can bend or straighten flower stems as needed for bouquets or arrangements.

GRID A series of squares made by attaching pieces of tape at right angles. Used to secure loose flowers in arrangements.

HANK A trade term used to describe a bunch of strings of identical beads sold as a unit. Usually six or more strands strung together form a hank.

HEAT-TRANSFER PAPER A specially treated paper with a waxy surface. An image is copied onto the waxy surface, and this can then be directly ironed onto smooth-surface fabrics. The fabric can be washed normally and the image will not be damaged.

HOT-GLUE GUN An electronic heating device shaped like a gun used to warm a stick of glue and apply the glue. The glue used in a glue gun is a plastic adhesive that reaches full bonding strength within one minute after it has been applied.

HYDROFLUORIC ACID A chemical that is the active ingredient in glass-etching cream; it eats away the shiny outside layer of the glass to create an abraded or frosted surface.

JUMP RINGS Small metal rings used to attach objects such as charms to a loop or chain. The jump ring is opened with needlenose pliers.

MOD PODGE A colorless, odorless, water-based acrylic sealer/glue manufactured by the Plaid company. It is used primarily for decoupage.

MUSLIN An unfinished, unbleached natural cotton. Traditionally used by clothing designers to create patterns and available in a variety of weights.

NEEDLENOSE OR LONG-NOSE PLIERS Pliers with long pointed tips. Helpful for forming wire loops and gripping tiny objects.

OASIS A solid, water-absorbent sponge material used for floral arranging. Usually comes in bricks but can be purchased in other shapes such as wreaths and can be easily trimmed to fit any container. Available from florists-supply and crafts stores.

PUDDLE To form a "puddle" of fabric on the floor, as when draperies contain excess fabric (for this purpose).

PUTTY KNIFE Tool used to apply spackle or plaster to walls and ceiling.

RAFFIA A natural plant material that comes from the palm plant. Traditionally used as decoration in floral arrangements, it can be color-dyed and is an extremely popular alternative to ribbon.

SISAL Robust fiber used in manufacturing flooring or rope.

SPACKLE A compound available in either powdered or premixed paste form that is used to fill small cracks and holes in ceilings or walls. I recommend the premixed paste form.

STITCHLESS GLUE A washable fabric glue that is great for sticking on appliqués and fabric cutouts and doing stitchless sewing. Dries clear and flexible. Hand-wash only.

SWAG A decoration that hangs in a curve between two points like a festoon, usually representing a line of drapery or a garland of leaves, flowers, or fruit. It may also be a suspended decoration.

TILE CUTTER A tool resembling pliers that allows you to "nibble" away edges of tile, leaving a smooth flat edge. Available at most hardware stores and home improvement centers.

TILE GROUT The filler used between tiles to help keep them secure and in place.

X-ACTO KNIFE A razor-sharp tool held like a pen or pencil, used to cut paper or fabric very exactly.

RESOURCE GUIDE

The listings for national chain stores include the addresses and phone numbers for the stores' headquarters; call or write for catalogs or nearby locations.

ABC Carpet and Home
888 Broadway
New York, NY 10011
212-473-3000
candles, picture frames,glassware, glass bottles, sisal rugs, napkins, sheets

Anthropology
1801 Walnut Street
Philadelphia, PA 19103
215-564-2313
candles, picture frames, glassware

Aphrodisia
264 Bleeker Street
New York, NY 10014
212-989-6440
essential oils, dried flowers

Bed Bath & Beyond
110 Bi Country #114
Farmingdale, NY 11735
516-420-7050
candles, picture frames, glass bottles, curtain rods, drapery accessories, baking sheets, glass cake stands, sheets, sisal rugs

Ben Franklin Craft Stores
1605 South First Street
Willmar, MN 56201
888-449-3795
brushes, paints, glues, dried flowers, Oasis wreaths

Bloomingdale's
1000 Third Avenue
New York, NY 10022
212-705-3000
candles, picture frames, glassware, sheets, napkins, sisal rugs

Bill's Flower Market
816 Sixth Avenue
New York, NY
212-889-8154
floral supplies, Oasis wreaths, floral wire and tape, dried flowers

Calico Corners
203 Gale Lane
Kennett Square, PA 19348
800-213-6366
muslin, assorted fabrics

Chambers (catalog)
P.O. Box 7841
San Francisco, CA 94120
800-334-9790
sheets, glass bottles

Crate & Barrel (catalog services)
646 N. Michigan Avenue
Chicago, IL 60611
312-787-5900
candles, glassware, glass bottles, napkins, sisal rugs

Eastern Art Glass
(makers of Armor Etch)
P.O. Box 9
Wyckoff, NJ 07481
800-872-3458
acid etching cream

Home Depot
449 Robert Court Road
Kennesaw, GA
404-433-8211
tools, glue, sisal rugs

Kinko's
255 West Stanley Avenue
Ventura, CA 93002
800-254-6567
color laser copies

Michael's Craft Store
8000 Bent Branch Drive
Irving, TX 75063
972-409-1538
brushes, paints, glues, dried flowers, Oasis
wreaths, floral tape, charms, jump rings

M. & J. Trimming
1008 Sixth Avenue
New York, NY 10018
212-391-9072
beads, ribbon, trimmings, charms,
jump rings

Pearl Paint (store and catalog)
308 Canal Street
New York, NY 10013
800-221-6843
art supplies, brushes, paints, paper, glues,
crackle medium, gold leaf, Wunda Size

Pier 1 Imports
P.O. Box 961020
Fort Worth, TX 76161
800-447-4371
candles, picture frames, glassware,
glass bottles, sisal rugs

Plaid Enterprises, Inc.
(makers of Mod Podge)
P.O. Box 7600
Norcross, GA 30091
800-842-4197
adhesives

Pottery Barn
100 Northpoint Street
San Francisco, CA 94133
415-421-7960
candles, picture frames, glassware,
glass bottles, sisal rugs

Staples
One Research Drive
Westboro, MA 01581
800-333-3330
decorative paper, heat-transfer paper

Visual Communications
300 Tristate International,
Suite 190
Lincolnshire, IL 60069
800-624-4210
heat-transfer paper

Williams-Sonoma
150 Northpoint Street
San Francisco, CA 94133
415-421-7900
glassware, glass bottles, napkins, tablecloths

Flea Markets

26th Street and 6th Avenue
New York, NY
212-243-5343

All-American Trade Day
11190 U.S. Highway 413
(between Albertville and Gunterville)
Gunterville, AL
205-891-2790
Held on weekends year-round.

Aloha Flea Market
9500 Salt Lake Boulevard
(in the parking lot of Aloha Stadium)
Honolulu, HI
808-730-9611
Held every Wednesday, Saturday,
and Sunday.

American Park 'n' Swap
40th Street and Washington Street
Phoenix, AZ
602-273-1258
Held every Wednesday evening, Friday,
Saturday, and Sunday.

Anderson Jockey Lot and Farmer's Market
Highway 29 between Greenville and
Anderson
Anderson, SC
864-224-2027
Held on weekends year-round.

The Annex Antiques Fair and Flea Market
6th Avenue and 27th Street
New York, NY
212-243-5343
Held every Saturday and Sunday
year-round.

Brimfield Antiques and Collectibles
Route 20
Brimfield, MA
413-245-3436
Held the first week of May, July,
and September.

Broad Acres Swap Meet
2960 Las Vegas Boulevard North
(at Pecos Street)
North Las Vegas, NV
702-642-3777
Held every Friday, Saturday,
and Sunday year-round.

Englishtown Auction Sales
90 Wilson Avenue
Englishtown, NJ
732-446-9644
Held every Saturday and Sunday
year-round as well as on special holidays
and the five days before Christmas.

The Flea Market
5225 East Platte Avenue (Highway 24)
Colorado Springs, CO
719-380-8599
Held every Saturday and Sunday
year-round as well as Fridays from
June through September.

Flea Market at Eastern Market
7th Street, SE at Eastern Market
(half block from Pennsylvania Avenue
on Capitol Hill)
Washington, DC
703-534-7612
Held Sundays from March
through Christmas.

Fort Lauderdale Swap Shop
Sunrise Boulevard one mile west of I-95
Fort Lauderdale, FL
954-791-7927
Held every day year-round from
6 A.M. to 6 P.M.

French Market Community Flea Market
1235 North Peters Street
(Elysian Fields at the Mississippi River)
New Orleans, LA
504-596-3420
Held every day year-round.

The Garage
25th Street, between 6th and 7th Avenues
New York, NY
Held on weekends year-round.

The Grand Bazaar
25th Street, between 6th Avenue and
Broadway
New York, NY
Held on weekends year-round.

Hartville Flea Market
788 Edison (at Market)
Hartville, OH
330-277-9860
Held Mondays, Thursdays,and holiday
Saturdays, April through Christmas.

Hinckley Flea Market
803 Highway 48 at I-35 (look for
five large red-and-white buildings)
Hinckley, MN
320-384-9911
Held the first weekend in May
through the last weekend in September.

Jack Loeks' Flea Market
1400 28th Street SW (three miles west
of Route 131, in the Studio 28 parking lot)
Grand Rapids, MI
616-532-8218
Held weekends April through October.

Kane County Flea Market
Randall Road (between Routes 38
and 64, about 40 miles west of Chicago)
St. Charles, IL
630-377-2252
Held the first Saturday and Sunday
of every month.

Lakewood Antiques Market
2000 Lakewood Way
Atlanta, GA
404-622-4488
Held every Friday, Saturday, and Sunday,
on the second full weekend of each month.

Lambertville Antique Market
Route 29
Lambertville, NJ
609-397-0456

Long Beach Outdoor Antiques
and Collectibles Market
Veteran Boulevard at Lakewood Boulevard
Long Beach, CA
213-655-5703
Held the third Sunday of every month.

Mary's Ole Time Swap Meet
7905 Northeast 23rd Street
Oklahoma City, OK
405-427-0051
Held on weekends year-round.

Metrolina Expo
7100 North Statesville Road (off I-77)
Charlotte, NC
800-824-3770
Held every Friday through Sunday
year-round.

Picc-a-dilly Flea Market
796 West 13th Street (Lane County
Fairgrounds)
Eugene, OR
541-683-5589
Held every Sunday year-round, except July
and August. Call to verify specific dates.

P.S. 44
76th Street and Columbus Avenue
New York, NY
212-974-6302

Redwood Swap Meet
3600 Redwood Road
Salt Lake City, UT
801-973-6060
Held every Saturday and Sunday.

Reningers #2 Antiques Market
740 Noble Street
Kutztown, PA
717-385-0104
Held every Saturday year-round. Call for
special dates on Saturday and Sunday in
late April, late June, and late September.

The Rose Bowl Flea Market
Pasadena, CA
626-588-4411
Held the second Sunday of every month.

Route 70 Flea Market
117 Route 70
Lakewood, NJ

Saturday Market
3rd and E Streets
(across from the Hilton Hotel)
Anchorage, AK
907-276-7207
Held every Sunday from mid-May
through mid-September.

Soho Antiques and Flea Market
Corner of Grand Street and Broadway
New York, NY
212-682-2000

Sparks Flea Market
At the junction of old U.S. Highway 36
(Mission Road) and Route 7 (about halfway
between St. Joseph, MO, and Atchison, KS)
Sparks, KS
913-985-2411
Held three weekends a year: in early May,
early July, and over Labor Day.

Tennessee State Fairgrounds Flea Market
Wedgewood Avenue and Nolensville Road
(State Faigrounds)
Nashville, TN
615-262-5016
Held the fourth weekend of every month.

Trader Jack's Flea Market
North of Highway 55 on the Santa Fe
Opera Grounds
Santa Fe, NM
No telephone
Held Fridays, Saturdays, and Sundays
in spring, summer, and fall.

Trader's Village
7979 North Eldridge Parkway
(³/₁₀ a mile south of I-290)
Houston, TX
281-890-5500
Held every weekend year-round.

Woodbury Antiques and Flea Market
Route 6
Woodbury, CT
203-263-2841

Auctions

Dutch Auction
Mickleton, NJ
609-423-6800

Lubin Galleries Auction House
Chelsea Antiques Buliding, 10th Floor
110 East 25th Street
New York, NY
212-929-0909
Auctions held on Thursday evenings.

S & S Auction
Repaupo, NJ
800-343-4979

South Jersey Auction
Repaupo, NJ
609-467-4834

Tepper Galleries
110 East 25th Street
New York, NY
212-677-5300